P9-DNF-397

FISHERMAN
BIBLE STUDYGUIDES

Growing Through Life's Challenges

JAMES AND MARTHA
REAPSOME

SHAW BOOKS
an imprint of WATERBROOK PRESS

Growing Through Life's Challenges

A SHAW BOOK

PUBLISHED BY WATERBROOK PRESS

2375 Telstar Drive, Suite 160

Colorado Springs, Colorado 80920

A division of Random House, Inc.

All Scripture quotations, unless otherwise indicated, are taken from the *Holy Bible, New International Version®*. NIV®. Copyright © 1973, 1978, 1984 by International Bible Society. Used by permission of Zondervan Publishing House. All rights reserved.

ISBN 0-87788-381-5

Copyright © 1995, 2001 by James and Martha Reapsome

All rights reserved. No part of this book may be reproduced or transmitted in any form or by any means, electronic or mechanical, including photocopying and recording, or by any information storage and retrieval system, without permission in writing from the publisher.

SHAW BOOKS and its aspen leaf logo are trademarks of WaterBrook Press, a division of Random House, Inc.

Printed in the United States of America

2003

21 20 19 18 17 16 15 14 13 12

Contents

How to Use This Studyguide

F isherman studyguides are based on the inductive approach to Bible study. Inductive study is discovery study; we discover what the Bible says as we ask questions about its content and search for answers. This is quite different from the process in which a teacher *tells* a group *about* the Bible—what it means and what to do about it. In inductive study God speaks directly to each of us through his Word.

A group functions best when a leader keeps the discussion on target, but the leader is neither the teacher nor the "answer person." A leader's responsibility is to *ask*—not *tell*. The answers come from the text itself as group members examine, discuss, and think together about the passage.

There are four kinds of questions in each study. The first is an *approach question*. Asked and answered before the Bible passage is read, this question breaks the ice and helps you start thinking about the topic of the Bible study. It begins to reveal where thoughts and feelings need to be transformed by Scripture.

Some of the early questions in each study are *observation questions*—who, what, where, when, and how—designed to help you learn some basic facts about the passage of Scripture.

Once you know what the Bible says, you then need to ask, *What does it mean?* These *interpretation questions* help you to discover the writer's basic message.

Next come *application questions*, which ask, *What does it mean to me?* They challenge you to live out the Scripture's life-transforming message.

Fisherman studyguides provide spaces between questions for jotting down responses as well as any related questions you would like to raise in the group. Each group member should have a copy of the studyguide and may take a turn in leading the group.

A group should use any accurate, modern translation of the Bible such as the *New International Version,* the *New American Standard Bible,* the *New Revised Standard Version,* the *New Jerusalem Bible,* or the *Good News Bible.* (Other translations or paraphrases of the Bible may be referred to when additional help is needed.) Bible commentaries should not be brought to a Bible study because they tend to dampen discussion and keep people from thinking for themselves.

Suggestions for Group Leaders

1. Thoroughly read and study the Bible passage before the meeting. Get a firm grasp on its themes and begin applying its teachings for yourself. Pray that the Holy Spirit will "guide you into all truth" (John 16:13) so that your leadership will guide others.

2. If any of the studyguide's questions seem ambiguous or unnatural to you, rephrase them, feeling free to add others that seem necessary to bring out the meaning of a verse.

3. Begin (and end) the study promptly. Start by asking someone to pray that every participant will both understand the passage and be open to its transforming power. Remember, the Holy Spirit is the teacher, not you!

4. Ask for volunteers to read the passages aloud.

5. As you ask the studyguide's questions in sequence, encourage everyone to participate in the discussion. If some are silent, try gently suggesting, "Let's have an answer from someone who hasn't spoken up yet."

6. If a question comes up that you can't answer, don't be afraid to admit that you're baffled. Assign the topic as a research project for someone to report on next week, or say, "I'll do some studying and let you know what I find out."

7. Keep the discussion moving, but be sure it stays focused. Though a certain number of tangents are inevitable, you'll want to quickly bring the discussion back to the topic at hand. Also, learn to pace the discussion so that you finish the lesson in the time allotted.

8. Don't be afraid of silences; some questions take time to answer, and some people need time to gather courage to speak. If silence persists, rephrase your question, but resist the temptation to answer it yourself.

9. If someone comes up with an answer that is clearly illogical or unbiblical, ask for further clarification: "What verse suggests that to you?"

10. Discourage overuse of cross references. Learn all you can from the passage at hand, while selectively incorporating a few important references suggested in the studyguide.

11. Some questions are marked with a ✎. This indicates that further information is available in the Leader's Notes at the back of the guide.

12. For further information on getting a new Bible study group started and keeping it functioning effectively, read *You Can Start a Bible Study Group* by Gladys Hunt and *Pilgrims in Progress: Growing Through Groups* by Jim and Carol Plueddemann. (Both books are available from Shaw Books.)

SUGGESTIONS FOR GROUP MEMBERS

1. Learn and apply the following ground rules for effective Bible study. (If new members join the group later, review these guidelines with the whole group.)

2. Remember that your goal is to learn all that you can *from the Bible passage being studied.* Let it speak for itself without using Bible commentaries or other Bible passages. There is more than enough in each assigned passage to keep your group productively occupied for one session. Sticking to the passage saves the group from insecurity ("I don't have the right reference books—or the time to read anything else.") and confusion ("Where did that come from? I thought we were studying _____.").

3. Avoid the temptation to bring up those fascinating tangents that don't really grow out of the passage you are discussing. If the topic is of common interest, you can bring it up later in informal conversation after the study. Meanwhile, help one another stick to the subject.

4. Encourage one another to participate. People remember best what they discover and verbalize for

themselves. Some people are naturally shy, while others may be afraid of making a mistake. If your discussion is free and friendly and you show real interest in what group members think and feel, the quieter ones will be more likely to speak up. Remember, the more people involved in a discussion, the richer it will be.

5. Guard yourself from answering too many questions or talking too much. Give others a chance to share their ideas. If you are one who participates easily, discipline yourself by counting to ten before you open your mouth.

6. Make personal, honest applications and commit yourself to letting God's Word change you.

Growing a Stronger Faith

God never promises to exempt Christians from common human experiences such as rejection, loss, grief, depression, failure, weakness, doubts, and injustice. If he did we might choose God just to avoid pain. Instead, God asks us to trust and love him in every situation because of who he is and how he loves us.

Life's challenges can strengthen our faith if we face them as the people in these studies did. As we explore their stories, we will discover their honest cries of pain and fear, their frustrations with their situations and with God, their mistakes and failures. But in the midst of the worst situation, we will also find God's repeated assurance: "I hear you. I am with you."

We pray that these studies will enable you to follow the example of those who faced their challenges honestly and grew in their faith and love for God.

Growing Through Rejection

SELECTIONS FROM EXODUS 2–5

The consequences of rejection explode on our television screens every day. A rejected suitor shoots his girlfriend. A rejected employee kills his boss. A rejected child commits suicide. Generally speaking, society does not handle rejection very well. Many people, because of their past failures, feel that God has rejected them. They quit trying to please him, and they launch into various kinds of destructive attitudes and behaviors.

It is important to study rejection from a biblical perspective. We need to find healthier and more appropriate ways to accept rejection and move beyond it, so that our lives are not destroyed.

Many of history's most successful leaders overcame rejection. Moses was one of them. This study will show how God used the pain of rejection to prepare Moses for leadership.

1. Describe the emotions you feel when you are rejected.

READ EXODUS 2:11-15.

⚲ 2. What do you think motivated Moses to intervene in the Egyptians' abusive treatment of the Hebrews?

in the fight between the two Hebrews?

3. What was the Hebrews' response to Moses? How would you feel if you had tried to right an injustice and your efforts were rejected?

Note: For forty years, Moses is isolated from his people and works as a shepherd in Midian, east of the Sinai Desert and the Red Sea. God appears to Moses and calls him to deliver the Hebrews from their slavery in Egypt. When Moses asks God his name, God replies, "I Am," or "The Lord." When Moses protests that he doesn't speak well enough to lead the people, God assigns his brother Aaron to help him.

⚲ *Indicates further information in Leader's Notes*

READ EXODUS 4:27–5:21.

 4. What would Aaron's coming to meet Moses mean
 to each of them because of their new assignments
 (4:27-28)?

 5. How do you account for the people's response to
 Moses and Aaron (4:29-31)?

 How would their response begin to heal the pain of
 rejection Moses had faced forty years before?

6. Describe how the Hebrews' situation gets worse after Moses and Aaron tell Pharaoh to let the people go.

Why would this new rejection by the Hebrews (5:19-21) be harder for Moses to deal with? (See also 4:29-31.)

READ EXODUS 5:22–6:8.

7. How did Moses respond to this new repudiation by the people he came to help (5:22-23)?

8. What do you learn from Moses about how to deal with rejection and other kinds of opposition?

✐ 9. In answer to Moses' accusations against him, how does God identify himself?

his past actions?

his future actions?

10. What did God say about who is really in charge in this situation: Pharaoh, Moses, or God?

11. What new perspective did God's statement in 6:6-8 give to Moses?

12. When you face rejection, what difference would it make to you to know that God hears, remembers, and is in charge? Why?

Pray the Bible into Life

- Thank God that you can honestly confess to him your fears of being rejected as well as your experience of rejection.
- Ask God to give you his perspective on your situation, to help you learn what you need to learn, and to help you trust him in the pain.
- Thank God that he is in charge of your past, present, and future.
- If you are in a group, pray for anyone who is currently facing the pain of rejection.

Growing Through Overwhelming Responsibilities

JOSHUA 1:1-11; 5:13–6:5; 23:1-16

A television commercial for a headache remedy begins with a vivid description of a housewife's overwhelming responsibilities: the kids are sick, the husband slams the door as he leaves for work, mounds of dirty dishes and clothes have piled up, and then a fuse blows. We chuckle at the poor woman's dilemma, but we have to admit that we ourselves often feel overwhelmed by our responsibilities and succumb to complaints, criticism, and despair. No pill can change that.

Part of the problem is that our culture tells us we are supposed to feel happy and fulfilled all the time. We are given no allowances, no exceptions, no middle ground. Deep down, however, we feel sure that our Christian faith must give us *some* answers to help us cope when we feel overwhelmed by life's demands. That's one reason the Bible includes stories of people like Joshua, who were thrust into seemingly impossible responsibilities. God handed his people, the Israelites, over to

Joshua just after Moses, their great liberator, had died. On the verge of conquering the Promised Land, the people were leaderless.

God called Joshua to assume command. Joshua would have crumbled under the load had it not been for God's intervention and Joshua's obedience.

1. How do overwhelming responsibilities affect you physically?

   emotionally?

   mentally?

   spiritually?

READ JOSHUA 1:1-11.

✍ 2. Imagine being in Joshua's position. What fears and doubts might you have had in this situation?

Why is God's message especially appropriate for Joshua at this time?

3. Three times God repeats his command to be strong and courageous. For what different responsibilities would Joshua need strength and courage (verses 6-9)?

✍ 4. What role was God's Law to have in Joshua's work?

Why does success for Joshua, and for us, depend on obedience to God rather than on our own strength, resources, or skills?

5. God knew what Joshua felt under his heavy load of responsibilities. What do God's words in verse 9 mean to you when you feel overwhelmed?

6. What does Joshua's response in verses 10-11 reveal about his courage and faith?

READ JOSHUA 5:13–6:5.

7. After safely crossing the Jordan River, the Israelites camp in sight of the walled city of Jericho, the next obstacle to occupying the land God promised to give them. Before the first big battle, what do you think would have been going through Joshua's mind?

✐ 8. What do you learn about the man with the drawn
    sword from his conversation with Joshua?

9. Why did Joshua need this encounter *before* God
    gave him instructions for doing the impossible?

    In what ways has God reminded you of his presence
    and involvement in your critical moments?

READ JOSHUA 23:1-16.

10. How do Joshua's instructions to the next generation
    (verses 6-11) compare with God's first instructions
    to him (1:6-9)?

11. At the end of his life, after faithfully leading Israel to occupy the land, Joshua summoned the leaders. What did Joshua want them to remember about the past (verses 3,9-10)?

What commands did he give in verses 6-11? Why these?

What warnings are outlined in verses 12-16? Why?

12. From Joshua's experience and wisdom, what do you learn about how to face overwhelming responsibilities?

13. What do you need to remember from the past about God's faithfulness and promises?

Which of the commands in verses 6-11 is most appropriate to your needs today?

Pray the Bible into Life

- Thank God that he knows your situation and your fears.
- Worship God for his holiness, his power, and his faithfulness to his promises.
- Ask God to help you love and obey him as you face your responsibilities in his strength.

Growing Through Doubts

JUDGES 6–7

When is doubt dangerous? When is it a healthy skepticism? If a securities salesman "guarantees" you a 15 percent return on your money, you'd better have some healthy skepticism. But we can't live with unresolved doubts indefinitely. We have to face them and deal with them courageously. If we don't we could develop ulcers, or worse. Doubts also assail us in our walk with God. They gnaw at our faith in God's integrity, love, wisdom, and power. If we do not handle our doubts positively, as Gideon did, we risk losing spiritual dividends. We have to look at doubt as a challenge to grow, not as an invitation to fail.

God instructed the Israelites to drive out all the pagan nations in Canaan. But after Joshua died, the next generation made them servants, intermarried with them, and worshiped their idols. When the Israelites suffered the consequences of their disobedience, they cried to God, who graciously raised up judges to free them from their oppressors. Gideon considered himself the least likely candidate for being a judge or mighty warrior. We can identify with Gideon as he struggled with doubts about God and himself.

1. Think of a time when you had doubts about God's will for you. How did you handle your doubts?

READ JUDGES 6:1-32.

⚙ 2. Describe the extent of the Israelites' economic and psychological oppression by the Midianites (verses 1-6).

⚙ 3. When the impoverished Israelites cried to the Lord for help, God sent a prophet who explained that the people were to blame for their troubles because they had forgotten God's goodness and had turned to idols. What does the angel's surprise appearance and message to Gideon indicate about God (verses 11-16)?

✗ 4. What doubts did Gideon have about God and
about himself (verses 12-15)? Why?

✗ 5. In what situations have you said: "If the Lord is
with us, why…?"; "But the Lord has abandoned
us…"; or "How can *I* do that…?"

✗ 6. Instead of chiding Gideon for his doubts, how did
God encourage Gideon's faith (verses 16-24)?

✐ 7. Before Gideon faced the army of Midian, God
      asked him to act against idolatry in his own family
      and village. If you were Gideon, what would you be
      saying to yourself and to your servants as you set out
      at night to do this risky thing (verses 25-27)?

8. What evidence does Gideon accumulate that
    showed God was with him (verses 23-24,28-32)?

READ JUDGES 6:33-40.

9. Gideon's response to the new invasion of the eastern
    armies was a mixture of faith and doubt. How did
    he demonstrate faith? doubt?

⌦ 10. Gideon wanted to obey God but was plagued with a doubt, "Will you save Israel by my hand?" How did God graciously reassure a hesitant Gideon that he was with him?

How has God graciously assured *you* that he is with you in times of uncertainty?

READ JUDGES 7:1-25.

⌦ 11. How does God reduce Gideon's army from thirty-two thousand to three hundred (verses 1-8)? Why?

12. How does God accommodate Gideon's doubts while still pushing him to act in faith (verses 8-15)?

✎ 13. What do you learn from Gideon about dealing with your doubts?

14. What do you learn about God from the way he related to Gideon and his doubts?

Pray the Bible into Life

- Thank God that he knows your doubts and fears. Ask him to help you see yourself and your situation from his point of view.
- Thank God for taking your doubts seriously and for offering you evidence about himself to encourage your faith.
- Ask God to make you willing to obey him even when you are afraid.

Growing Through Loss and Grief

SELECTIONS FROM JOB

S everal years ago we took an evening class called "Death and Other Endings." Death is the most commonly feared ending, but we also discussed other "endings": leaving home, losing a job, divorce, losing health or independence. All of these losses cause us pain, grief, anger, resentment, despair, loneliness, or isolation.

When the professor asked us to explore possible positive outcomes from our losses and grief, a number of amazing insights, new possibilities, and new beginnings emerged from some of the students' stories. But others angrily rejected the possibility of any positive outcome and grew more isolated from the class.

In the Bible, Job experienced a staggering series of tragic losses. But he faced them in a way that strengthened his relationship with God and allowed for new beginnings.

1. In her book *Early Widow,* Mary Jane Worden shares her discovery that grieving leads to healing. As part

of the grieving process, she encourages anyone facing grief to:

- face it, name it, allow yourself to feel the sadness
- acknowledge your loss, talk about it, don't run away from it
- allow God to comfort you

What parts of this process have brought healing to you, or to a friend, in grief?

READ JOB 1:1–2:10.

✐ 2. What impresses you about Job's character and his position in the community?

✐ 3. What different kinds of losses does Job suffer?

Give modern-day equivalents to Job's losses. What would these kinds of losses look like today?

🖉 4.   When you suffer grief and loss, what temptations often accompany them?

5.   What is Job's initial response to these devastating losses and the accompanying temptations (1:20-22; 2:9-10)? Why do you think he reacted that way?

READ JOB 3:20-26.

Three friends of Job come to comfort him but are so moved by the sight of him that they sit silently for seven days. Finally, Job begins to speak, cursing the day of his birth and wishing he had never been born.

✐ 6.   What do you learn of the depth of Job's pain from the words he used to describe his grief?

What emotional impact do these words have on you?

✐ 7.   When facing grief, a Christian may feel compelled to say, "The Lord gave and the Lord has taken away; may the name of the Lord be praised" (1:21). But most of us would hesitate to quote 3:20-26. What healthy steps did Job take to talk honestly about his pain?

READ JOB 23:10-17.

Job's friends—assuming that trouble is punishment for the wicked—condemned Job for some secret sin. Job insisted that if he could only find God and question him, God, as a just judge, would vindicate him.

8. How did Job describe his own righteousness (verses 10-12)?

⬦ 9. Job longed for an explanation from God about why a righteous person like himself should suffer such calamity. What conflicting ideas about God trouble Job (verses 10-17)?

10. Job was confident that God's purpose was not to destroy him, but to refine him as gold (verse 10). How can such confidence in God's character and purpose comfort you during times of grief?

Read Job 40:1-5; 42:1-6.

Instead of explaining Job's situation or finding any moral fault with Job, God questioned him: "Where were you when I created the world? Can you command the constellations and all of nature? Do you send lightning bolts on their way? Can you act like God?" (chapters 38–40).

⚘ 11. Why did Job have nothing to say in the presence of God (40:3-5)?

⚘ 12. Of what did Job need to repent (42:2-6)?

Did Job need to be humbled? Why or why not? (See 23:10-12.)

13. Why was God himself, not explanations or arguments, the source of comfort for Job? How is he your source of comfort when you suffer loss?

Pray the Bible into Life

- Thank God for who he is: your wise, loving, just, and powerful Creator and Judge.

- Confess your honest feelings of grief to God as well as the temptation to doubt his character rather than trusting his goodness.

- Thank God that he can use your grief to show you more of who he is, to purify you, and to make you more like the Lord Jesus.

Growing Through Being in the Middle

SELECTIONS FROM 1 SAMUEL 18–23

Y our son has come up with an exciting plan. As many children do, he goes to Mom first, and she says, "Okay, but check with your father." Then he comes to you, bubbling with enthusiasm. But when you hear his scheme, you hesitate. "But Mom says it's okay," he pleads. The trap of being in the middle snaps shut and you are caught.

Parents can't dodge the trap. Neither can a pastor when two parishioners bring a dispute to him. Nor can supervisors on the job. You may even wander into a no-man's land between two feuding friends.

Welcome to one of life's tough challenges, one that God knows all about and helps us to endure, just as he helped Jonathan, the son of King Saul. God rejected Saul, the first king of Israel, after Saul rejected the word of the Lord. When it became evident that God was with David, Saul became jealous and fearful of David. But Jonathan loved and respected David.

1. What do you feel when you are caught in the middle of a problem between two people you love? How does a situation like this pull you in two different directions?

READ 1 SAMUEL 18:1-16,28-30.

2. What do you think are the reasons for Saul's jealousy of David?

READ 1 SAMUEL 19:1-10.

3. When Saul ordered his son Jonathan to kill David, what risks did Jonathan take for his friend (verses 1-7)?

4. What effects might Saul's unpredictable behavior toward David have had on Jonathan (verses 6-10)?

READ I SAMUEL 20:1-42.

 5. After fleeing for his life, David secretly returned to appeal to Jonathan for help. What different perspectives do David and Jonathan have concerning Saul (verses 1-9)?

6. Describe the plan Jonathan devised to inform David of Saul's intentions (verse 10-23).

✐ 7. What will it cost Jonathan if God does what Jonathan anticipated in verses 13-17?

8. David and Jonathan both recognized that God was involved in their situation (verses 8,22-23). How would recognizing God's interest in your situation help you cope with being in the middle?

✐ 9. Imagine yourself as Jonathan. What emotional ups and downs would you have faced during the New Moon festival (verses 24-34)?

Describe similar roller-coaster emotions you've faced when you've been caught in the middle.

✐ 10. Saul and Jonathan both saw the other's behavior as shameful (verses 30-31,34). Why is shame such a devastating accusation when you are trying to do what is right?

11. When Jonathan realized he must send David away, what different sorrows caused each man to weep (verse 41)?

READ I SAMUEL 23:15-18.

12. When David was hiding, Jonathan came, probably at their last meeting, to help David find strength in God (verse 16). How would his actions and his words have accomplished that purpose?

When you have been the person who is estranged, as David was, how has a friend in the middle helped you find strength in God?

13. What do you learn from Jonathan's courage, risk taking, and confidence in God that can help you when you are caught in the middle of uncomfortable circumstances?

Pray the Bible into Life

- Thank the Lord Jesus, your advocate before God, for understanding what it means to be in the middle.
- Thank God that just as he completely understood the motives of the three parties involved in the biblical account, he completely understands each of our motives, even when we misjudge one another.
- Confess your fears and pain about being in the middle and pray for wisdom for one another in these situations.

Growing Through Facing Sin

2 SAMUEL 11:1-27; 12:1-14; PSALM 51

W hile visiting friends in another city, we decided to go to a church where we knew the pastor and his wife. We approached them with some apprehension after the service because it was the first time we had seen them since he had confessed to adultery and resigned as president of a Christian organization. He had withdrawn from the ministry for several years and accepted counseling from older, respected pastors. We greeted each other warmly and chatted for a few minutes. It was quite clear that his congregation appreciated his ministry. Why? Because this man had faced his sin, confessed it to God and his peers, accepted God's forgiveness, and made a fresh start. He had followed in the footsteps of King David.

1. When people are caught cheating, lying, defrauding, or stealing materials from their company, what are their most common responses?

✐ Read 2 Samuel 11:1-27.

✐ 2. Trace the steps in David's temptation and the choices he made that compounded his sin and guilt.

3. In what ways were other people affected by David's sin?

Bathsheba

the messengers

Uriah

Joab

other soldiers

God

✐ 4.   How have ease or self-confidence made you
        vulnerable to temptation like David?

READ 2 SAMUEL 12:1-14.

5. In what sense was Nathan a messenger of God's mercy as well as God's judgment?

↗ 6. What were David's options after Nathan confronted him?

Why is David's confession in verse 13 the only proper response, or hope, when you face your own guilt?

✐ 7. Forgiveness wipes out the guilt but not the consequences of sinful choices. What consequences did David's sin bring to himself, his family, and the nation (verses 10-14)?

READ PSALM 51.

✐ 8. David wrote this psalm after Nathan confronted him about his sin. What specific things did David ask God to do for him (verses 1-12)?

What do David's requests reveal about sin's effect on us?

9. When someone is caught in a wrongful act, a common response is to blame others or to blame circumstances. How does David resist these temptations to blame (verses 3-6)?

10. What kind of relationship does David long for with God that goes beyond just having a clean slate (verses 10-12)?

Which of these requests most fits your needs right now?

11. Of all the things David could have done to thank God for restoring him, why are a broken spirit and a contrite heart the appropriate sacrifices to offer (verses 13-17)?

⚘ 12. What kind of "sacrifices," other than a broken spirit
and a contrite heart, have you tried to offer God to
prove you're sorry?

13. In the Old Testament God often refers to "my servant David," not to "the murderer and adulterer
David." The way David faced his sin and guilt freed
him to enjoy God's forgiveness and to serve God
well. The New Testament instructs us how to follow
David's example: "If we claim to be without sin, we
deceive ourselves and the truth is not in us. If we
confess our sins, he is faithful and just and will for-
give us our sins and purify us from all unrighteous-
ness. If we claim we have not sinned, we make him
out to be a liar and his word has no place in our
lives" (1 John 1:8-10). What did you learn from this
study about how to grow spiritually through facing
your sin and guilt?

Pray the Bible into Life

- Thank God that he is not surprised or shocked by what he sees in your heart, although some of it shocks you.
- Ask God to help you confess your sin and guilt honestly, instead of denying or blaming others.
- Pray those requests in Psalm 51 that express what you want God to do for you.

STUDY 7

Growing Through Depression and Anger

SELECTIONS FROM JEREMIAH

Charles Spurgeon, England's most famous preacher in the late 19th century, is probably the most quoted man in America's pulpits on any given Sunday. Preachers love his colorful stories and practical insights. What we're not told, however, is how much Spurgeon suffered from depression. He often warned those he taught to watch out for Mondays when they likely would be plunged into despair from the heights of exaltation on Sundays.

Depression is no stranger to many Christians. It often leads to anger at God, which results in guilt feelings, which leaves us more depressed, and then the cycle repeats itself. We feel as if we're being strangled to death by a python. The prophet Jeremiah felt like that too, and he got angry with God. God met him at his lowest point, and Jeremiah returned to his calling with courage and faith.

1. Why do Christians so rarely admit or talk openly about depression?

READ JEREMIAH 1:4-10,17-19.

✎ 2. What were the various factors involved in God's call to Jeremiah to be his prophet?

✎ 3. What did God command Jeremiah to do (verses 9-10)?

What might be the consequences for Jeremiah if he obeyed God's command?

4. What did God promise to do for Jeremiah when he began to experience opposition to his ministry (verses 17-19)?

✐ 5. How does a realistic assessment of your problems and of God's resources help you deal with discouragement or depression?

READ JEREMIAH 11:18-23.

6. Jeremiah's hometown was Anathoth (1:1). What is the response of his fellow townspeople to his preaching (verses 19,21)?

How might the reaction of his hometown have contributed to Jeremiah's depression?

7. Why does criticism from our peers and even our family members bother us so much?

READ JEREMIAH 12:1-5.

✎ 8. Jeremiah became angry over God's apparent injustice. What effect does his anger have on his attitude toward the wicked (verses 3-4)?

✎ 9. God answered Jeremiah with vivid questions about surviving in more challenging situations (verse 5). What principle of spiritual growth did God want to teach Jeremiah?

READ JEREMIAH 15:15-21.

🖋 10. What evidence of Jeremiah's deep depression do you find in verses 15-18?

🖋 11. Why did God call Jeremiah to repent (verse 19)?

12. Of what value was it to Jeremiah to be reminded of God's original promise of protection (verses 20-21 and 1:17-19)?

READ JEREMIAH 20:7-18.

🖋 13. After being beaten and imprisoned, Jeremiah continued to preach judgment on Judah (see 20:1-6). Describe his emotional roller-coaster ride, his lows and highs.

Note: Later, Jeremiah's writings are burned (chapter 36), he is imprisoned (chapter 37), he is thrown into a cistern to die (chapter 38), and his wise counsel is rejected (42:1-6; 43:1-7). His preaching fails to save Judah and Jerusalem. However, after Jeremiah's outburst in chapter 20, we find no further signs of anger, depression, or complaints about God's dealings.

✐ 14. Jeremiah spilled out his anger, resentment, and depression to God. As he listened to God, Jeremiah changed his attitude toward his circumstances and toward God. In what ways can Jeremiah's example help you deal with depression and anger toward God?

Pray the Bible into Life

- Ask God to help you be more realistic and honest about depression, anger toward him, and discouragement.
- Pray for boldness to talk to God about these things, just as Jeremiah did.
- Seek God's grace and power to overcome at least one cause of depression, anger, or discouragement in your life.

Growing Through Pressure to Compromise

DANIEL 6

D uring the dark days of World War II, compromisers sold out to Hitler and jeopardized the lives of the resistance fighters, who were known as the Fifth Column in France and Quislings in Norway. Those names became synonymous with traitorous conduct that compromised the values of freedom and liberty in exchange for dictatorship and bondage. On the other hand, in Holland many Christians, such as Corrie ten Boom, could have compromised the lives of Jewish refugees, but they didn't. Instead, they risked their own lives to hide these refugees. Daniel was like that. He refused to compromise his faith in God even when facing certain death.

1. In what situations today are people pressured to compromise their Christian values and practices?

READ DANIEL 6:1-14.

✎ 2. Why did the king's changes in administration cause trouble for Daniel (verses 1-5)?

3. Daniel's integrity, hard work, and moral example did not exempt him from attack. What issues were behind the administrators' attack on Daniel's faith?

✎ 4. What aspects of your faith and character might be evident to your coworkers?

5. Why do you think Darius agreed to issue the decree the leaders requested (verses 6-9)?

⚴ 6. Imagine yourself as Daniel. After hearing about the decree, how would you have decided what to do (verses 10-11)?

7. What difference does it make in your praying when you realize that God alone can help you (verse 11)?

⚴ 8. The leaders were sure they had the perfect trap when they asked the king about his decree and then announced that Daniel had broken it. What might Darius have been feeling as he tried to find a way out of the trap he created (verses 12-14)?

What might this day have been like for Daniel?

READ DANIEL 6:15-28.

9. As the decree is carried out, what did Darius recognize about Daniel and Daniel's God (verse 16)?

10. At dawn Darius rushed to the lions' den with one question, "Daniel, servant of the living God, has your God, whom you serve continually, been able to rescue you from the lions?" (verse 20). What, if anything, does your reaction to difficult circumstances prompt your coworkers or neighbors to ask you about your God?

What additional insights do you gain from Colossians 4:5-6 and 1 Peter 2:11-17?

11. The king was overjoyed when Daniel was lifted out of the den unharmed. What did Darius and the whole empire learn about God because of Daniel's faith (verses 23-27)?

12. The attack on Daniel was an opportunity for God to demonstrate his power. Daniel prospered, but for many of us it sometimes looks like the lions win. Christians lose jobs or are passed over for promotion because of their integrity, hard work, or moral example. How can maintaining your integrity at work and in your relationships, without compromise, demonstrate God's power?

Pray the Bible into Life

- Thank God that he fully understands both the pressure you feel to compromise and your desire to honor him.
- Ask God to help you live and work in ways that will make your coworkers and neighbors curious about your faith.
- If you are in a group, pray for one another to be able to withstand the pressure to compromise this week.

Growing Through Perplexing Situations

HABAKKUK 1–3

B est-selling author Thomas Moore, whose books *Care of the Soul* and *Soul Mates* point out the fallacy of quick-fix solutions for our problems, said in a magazine interview, "It's not necessary to get so burdened about everything turning out right." He said that in our intense efforts to improve ourselves, "we ignore the soul." If we try to run away from suffering, "then our pleasures will tend to be superficial as well" (*American Way,* June 15, 1994).

The prophet Habakkuk did not run away from pain or perplexity. When things in Judah seemed to go awry, he pleaded with God to straighten things out. In the end, he found satisfaction in his soul, not in being rescued, but in committing his questions to God's wisdom, love, and power.

1. When have you suddenly faced a situation that seemed unjust, impossible, or beyond understanding?

READ HABAKKUK 1:1–2:1.

2. What caused Habakkuk to question God about the society in Judah (1:1-4)?

the evils injustice that seemed to triumph

3. What questions do you ask God about your society?

very similar ??
why Lord

4. Why would God's answer have perplexed Habakkuk even more (1:5-11)?

the raise up an evil people seems intolerable at best

5. How did Habakkuk's understanding of God's character create more questions for him (1:12–2:1)?

how could god who knows all ; trust these people

6. Habakkuk determined to watch and wait for God's answer to his questions (2:1). Why is this an appropriate way for you to face perplexities as well?

This shows trust & faith in God let God do what is necessary. Real belief that Healing has power & strength

What difference does your faith make regarding how you wait for an answer from God or for a change in your circumstances?

the amount of faith & trust I have determines the amt. of worry and anxiety

READ HABAKKUK 2:2-20.

7. How might God's answer in verses 2-5 have stretched and encouraged Habakkuk's faith?

Just knowing God was listening would be encouraging. Knowing God cared about what troubled H and Had a plan to correct the sit

8. In contrast to the righteous who live by faith, how did the Babylonians live (verse 4-19)?

wickedly; greedy, drunkards

9. What does verse 14 say that puts the glory and power of the Babylonians and their idols into perspective?

God will prevail
Evil w/ be swallowed up

10. What difference does it make to look at an impossible situation in the light of verse 20?

the Lord will prevail — He is always available to us

READ HABAKKUK 3.

11. How does the tone of Habakkuk's prayer in this passage differ from the tone of his prayers in chapter 1?

In chapt 1 H. was angry & couldn't believe God wasn't doing anything
In chap. 3 H.

12. Habakkuk wrote his worst possible scenario in terms of the agricultural society of his time (verses 16-17). How would you rewrite these verses in terms of our society today?

13. How have God's power and mercy helped you wait patiently and rejoice in him in a perplexing situation?

Pray the Bible into Life

- Thank God that no circumstances take him by surprise or are outside his control.
- Confess your fears and doubts about the evil or injustice you face.
- Pray Habakkuk's prayer together:

> LORD, I have heard of your fame;
> I stand in awe of your deeds, O LORD.
> Renew them in our day,
> in our time make them known;
> in wrath remember mercy. (Habakkuk 3:2)

Growing Through Failure

SELECTIONS FROM MATTHEW 26; JOHN 21:1-19

Thomas Edison, America's most famous inventor, was responsible for about thirteen hundred inventions. Someone reminded him how many times he had failed trying to invent a new storage battery. He had made fifty thousand experiments before he got results. Edison dismissed the failures and said, "I know fifty thousand things that won't work."

The same principle applies to spiritual growth. We have to be able to look at our failures as steppingstones to success. If we give up on ourselves and on God's patient love, we will remain mired in old, unproductive habits. This study about Peter's failure and recovery gives us hope for spiritual progress.

1. What is the worst part of failure for you: disappointing yourself, breaking a promise, experiencing the consequences for yourself or others, or starting over?

READ MATTHEW 26:31-46.

   2. What do you learn in verses 31-35 about Peter's motives, his view of himself, and his view of the other disciples?

   3. Jesus confided his deep sorrow to Peter, James, and John, asking them to share this darkest hour with him. Imagine you are Peter. How would you have felt when Jesus questioned you (verses 36-41)?

   4. What indicates that the disciples did not realize the seriousness of this moment for themselves or for Jesus?

When have you misread a critical situation, not recognizing the need to pray or to be on guard against temptation?

READ MATTHEW 26:57-58,69-75.

5. Peter followed Jesus into the courtyard of the high priest. Why do you think he stayed when he was questioned instead of running away?

✐ 6. Describe how each accusation of Peter grew more threatening.

7. How did Peter make each of his denials stronger?

✐ 8. At the moment the rooster crowed, Peter realized what he had done. Why was his weeping a proper response?

If you have ever felt the way Peter must have felt, what would you be saying to yourself and to God?

READ JOHN 21:1-19.

9. After his resurrection Jesus appeared twice to the disciples in the Upper Room, showing them his wounds and convincing them he really was alive. Then he met them again by the Sea of Galilee. Why do you think Peter behaved the way he did in verses 7 and 10-11?

10. Why is it so important to be given an opportunity to please or to *do something right* after you have failed?

11. Thinking back on Peter's words to Jesus in the Upper Room (Matthew 26:33-35), what changes do you see in Peter in this private conversation with Jesus (verses 15-19)?

What do you think Jesus' questions and new assignment might have meant to Peter?

12. In starting over again after failure, why is each of the following steps necessary?
   a. Grieving over your failure

b. Knowing you are forgiven

c. Forgiving yourself

d. Rebuilding trust

e. Taking the opportunity to try again

Pray the Bible into Life

- Thank the Lord Jesus that he knows you better than you know yourself and is not shocked by your failures.
- Ask for persistence to watch and pray so that you will be prepared for temptation.
- Thank God for his mercy, his forgiveness, and the opportunity to start again.

Growing Through Weakness

2 CORINTHIANS 4:7-12,16-18; 12:7-10

F or the most part, the world celebrates strength and power and denigrates weakness. Society's search for power as a virtue is illustrated by Napoleon I. One day in school he had to stand under the flag of Carthage, a conquered city, while his older brother stood under the flag of Rome. Even though this was only a history lesson, he demanded to change places with his brother so he would not have to stand under the flag of the defeated.

Jesus' not standing up for himself looked like weakness, and his execution seemed a sure defeat. But out of this seeming weakness and defeat came ultimate victory and triumph through his resurrection. We need to learn this principle of strength through weakness, as the apostle Paul did.

1. Why are we afraid to admit weakness?

READ 2 CORINTHIANS 12:7-10.

2. In response to the false teachers' boasting, Paul listed
   his credentials, concluding with a vision he had of
   paradise. Instead of boasting of his special privileges
   and revelations, why does Paul boast about his
   weaknesses?

   That Christ's power would take over

3. How did Paul account for his thorn in the flesh?

   to keep him from becooming conceited

4. What insights does verse 8 give you into Paul's inner
   struggle with his weakness?

   *he didn't want the pain
   he pleaded w/ God to taken it away*

   3+5

5. In facing your weakness, what is the value of pleading with God for a specific request, then waiting, listening, and pleading again?

   *staying connected - having faith
   that He'll answer*

✐ 6. Imagine yourself in Paul's circumstances. How would you have responded to God's answer in verse 9?

I think I would have 1st wondered if I would be more effective if I were 100%

✐ 7. In what ways is Paul's response different from merely resigning himself to living with pain (verses 9-10)?

he's still depending on God to get help from through still expecting to serve

READ 2 CORINTHIANS 4:7-12,16-18.

✐ 8. List all of the illustrations you can find in this passage of Paul's statement in 2 Corinthians 12:10: "When I am weak, then I am strong."

Paul's weakness

crushed
perplexed
persecuted

God's power

uplifting
ever present

9. We tend to delight in our strength, achievements, power, or success as demonstrations of Christ's power in our lives. Describe a time when you have seen God's power demonstrated in *your* weakness?

When Dave was in hospital, I felt scared, inadequate, vulnerable in having to deal with family members. I was so overwhelmed I gave up control - knowing I couldn't stand alone

10. In what ways are Jesus' death and life being worked out in you daily at home, at work, and in your relationships (verses 10-12)?

neec

11. Paul didn't lose heart because he viewed his weakness from an eternal perspective. How did he show the contrasts between his present experience and eternal reality (verses 16-18)?

12. What difference can an eternal perspective make in the way you view your weaknesses and your anxieties?

externally one might get caught up in feelings of self-pity, defeat

Pray the Bible into Life

- Thank God that he knows and accepts your weaknesses even when you don't.
- Confess your fear or denial of weakness to God and ask for faith to believe that his strength is made perfect in your weakness.
- Thank God for the times his strength has been made perfect in your weakness and his grace has been sufficient for you or for someone in your group.

What Makes It All Possible?

PSALM 116

When our little boy got stuck in a tree, he wasted no time calling for help. His plaintive shouts brought us to the rescue. Why did he yell for his parents? Because he was in a jam and he knew from past experiences that we loved him, that we were strong enough to get him safely out of the tree, and that we would respond immediately. Our track record was infallible as far as he was concerned.

Many times the Christian's walk with God follows the same pattern. God loves to hear from his children when we face life's challenges, because our cries prove our faith in him. Our cries really are a confession of our own weakness and of God's strength. Each difficulty we face tests what we believe about where our security lies—in our own strength and ingenuity or in God's love and power. The psalmist passed the test.

1. How do you respond to someone who really listens to you, who hears your feelings as well as your words?

READ PSALM 116.

✐ 2. What did the psalmist do when he faced trouble (verses 1-11)?

✐ 3. What did God do in response to the simple, honest cries of this hurting believer (verses 1-2,5-8)?

✐ 4. The psalmist didn't give details of the challenge he faced, but Moses, Joshua, Gideon, Job, Jonathan, David, Jeremiah, Daniel, Habakkuk, Peter, and Paul could have identified with him. With what part of the psalmist's experience can you identify?

⌀ 5. The psalmist learned that God is gracious, right-eous, and full of compassion (verse 5). Why do you need God to be all of these things?

⌀ 6. Why do you think the simple-hearted qualify for God's protection (verse 6)?

⌀ 7. How did the psalmist's experience of God change his attitude toward death (verses 3,8,15)?

⌀ 8. How does an understanding of God's character relieve your fear of death?

9. Why did the psalmist's dismay tempt him to become cynical or bitter (verses 10-11)?

How have you handled this same temptation when facing difficulties?

⌀ 10. Because God heard him, the psalmist joyfully responded to God in several ways. With which of his responses do you most closely identify (verses 1,7,9,13,18-19)?

⌀ 11. Why are praising God, repeatedly calling on his name, and keeping your vows appropriate ways to repay him for his goodness to you (verse 12-14)?

12. What vows have you made to God (at your baptism, upon joining the church, in marriage, in private)?

13. You have examined eleven situations that challenged people in the Bible to grow in their faith through the way they faced specific difficulties. All of their testimonies could echo Psalm 116. What principles do you find in this psalm that can help you grow stronger through your challenges?

Pray the Bible into Life

- Thank God that he hears your cry for mercy and
  will deliver you from death, from tears, and from
  stumbling.
- Tell the Lord that you love him, and thank him
  for his good and gracious work in your life.
- If you are in a study group, consider the challenges currently facing the members of your
  group. Use parts of this psalm to pray for each
  other.

Leader's Notes

Study 1: Growing Through Rejection

Question 2. After Moses' Hebrew birth mother weaned him, Pharaoh's daughter raised him in the palace (Exodus 2:1-10). He lived between two cultures and didn't fit in either one.

Question 4. The mountain of God was Mount Horeb, also called Mount Sinai (Exodus 3:1,12; 19:1-2).

Question 9. If necessary, ask the group, "What other names do you find in verse…?" or "What other actions do you find in verse…?" Notice the references to time: Exodus 6:2-5, past; verses 6-8, future.

Study 2: Growing Through Overwhelming Responsibilities

Question 2. Use a Bible map to locate the territory that God gave to the Israelites: from the desert in the south to Lebanon in the north, from the Mediterranean Sea on the west to the Euphrates River on the east (Joshua 1:4).

Question 4. The Book of the Law in Joshua 1:8 refers to the commandments and instructions God gave to Moses in Exodus 20–23, which are also summarized in Deuteronomy.

Question 8. "This was an angel of superior rank, the commander of the Lord's army. Some say he was an appearance of

God in human form. As a sign of respect, Joshua took off his sandals. Although Joshua was Israel's leader, he was still subordinate to God, the absolute Leader" (*Life Application Bible,* Wheaton, Ill.: Tyndale House Publishers, 1990, p. 341). Israel wanted and expected God to be on their side. The angel's reply, "Neither" (Joshua 5:14), negates that expectation. God isn't someone we "get on our side" to do our will. "The covenant Lord is free to become an adversary (Hosea 13:8) or to allow Israel's adversaries to do their work (Joshua 7:1-5)" (E. John Hamlin, *Joshua Inheriting the Land,* Grand Rapids, MI: Eerdmans, 1983, p. 40). But the angel comes to instruct and comfort Joshua *now,* at this critical time.

Study 3: Growing Through Doubts

Question 2. The Midianites, living in the desert east of the Jordan River, were descendants of Abraham through Midian, son of the concubine Keturah. They planned annual invasions of Israel after the winter rains ended and the spring wheat and barley were ready to harvest. The Midianites ate off the land and trampled everything they did not use.

Gideon could not risk having the Midianites see him thresh wheat, so he stood in a winepress (Judges 6:11), a pit hidden from view. Normally farmers threshed wheat in a large open area so that as they tossed the beaten wheat into the air, the wind blew away the chaff and left only the wheat behind.

Question 3. The angel of the Lord is "an expression widely used in the Old Testament to denote Yahweh Himself in His manifestation to men. See Judges 6:11-24; 13:3-21" (*The New*

Bible Commentary Revised, Grand Rapids, Mich.: Eerdman's Publishing Co., 1970, p. 258).

Question 4. If necessary, follow up with, "How did the angel describe Gideon?" (Judges 6:12,14) and "How did Gideon describe himself?" (verses 13,15).

Question 5. Encourage honest answers, but don't pressure anyone to expose pain or doubts before he or she is ready.

Question 6. The Israelites' belief that to see God meant death was based on God's words to Moses: "You cannot see my face, for no one may see me and live" (Exodus 33:20).

Question 7. Baal was the Canaanite god who controlled agriculture. The Asherah pole honored the fertility goddess. In the Canaanite religion, successful crops depended on proper worship of these gods.

Question 10. Gideon might have recognized that the thick fleece could have absorbed dew, leaving the ground dry in comparison. To have the fleece dry would be an even surer sign.

Gideon's putting out the fleece shows one way God guided decision making (Judges 6:36-40). The results confirmed the will of God and led Gideon to victory over the Midianites. However, this experience is not God's model for guiding his children. Jesus said the Holy Spirit would guide his followers (John 14:26; 16:13), and the apostle Paul's ministry was guided by the Spirit (Acts 13:2; 16:6).

Question 11. Drinking water from the hand allowed a soldier to keep his head up so he could be alert to danger, which was much better than having his face in the stream. If the group isn't clear about why God reduced the army, you can ask, "Why would being self-sufficient dishonor God and be dangerous for a person of faith?"

Question 13. Encourage the group to review the story, tracing Gideon's steps from voicing his doubts to the angel to leading the army, shouting, "For the Lord and for Gideon."

Study 4: Growing Through Loss and Grief

Question 2. The origin of Job's suffering was God's question to Satan (Job 1:8; 2:3). Satan questioned Job's integrity by suggesting he feared God only for what he could get out of it himself (1:9-11). Then he suggested Job's faith would disappear if his own body were attacked ("skin for skin," 2:4-5). God knew Job's basic need was to see his supremacy in all things. Satan was used by God to accomplish his purposes for Job. God permitted Satan to do what he wanted, within certain limits (1:12; 2:6). After Satan had done his worst and Job had refused to curse God, the conversation between God and Satan ended.

Question 3. If the group needs help getting the details, you might ask, "What else do you see in verse…?" Job lost five hundred yoke of oxen, five hundred donkeys, three thousand camels and the herdsmen to invaders; he lost seven thousand sheep and their shepherds to lightning; he lost his seven sons and three daughters to a wind storm; he lost his health to painful sores; he lost the comfort and sympathy of his wife; and he lost the respect of his friends and of the community.

Question 4. Encourage the group to recall things they have been tempted to think, say, or do when facing loss, things that contradicted what they knew and believed about God.

Question 6. After the group has found all of the descriptions, you might reread Job's words and ask the group to consider how these descriptions affect them emotionally.

Question 7. You might compare these verses to the suggestions in question 1.

Question 9. Be sure the group gets the details. Ask, "Is there something else in verse...?"

Question 11. When Job sees God for who he is, Job has a different perspective on himself and his situation. In the presence of almighty God, our accusations and complaints are exposed for what they are.

Question 12. In Job 23:10-17, Job was sure of his righteousness compared to other people. He was the best person he knew. But in waiting for God's response, Job learns to see himself from God's point of view, and so do we.

STUDY 5: GROWING THROUGH BEING IN THE MIDDLE

Question 3. Throughout this study, try to put yourself in Jonathan's place. Imagine how you would feel if your father commanded you to murder your best friend. Imagine the thoughts Jonathan must have had and the options he must have considered.

Question 5. Being emotionally connected to someone makes it hard to be objective about them or their behavior. We can overreact and see no good in them, as David did with Saul, or we can become overly protective of them in spite of their destructive behavior, as Jonathan did in this passage.

Question 7. It was common at this time for a new king to completely destroy the family of the previous ruler. Imagine you are Jonathan speaking about your father and your family, and recognizing that God will destroy every one of David's enemies. Consider the implications of these things from Jonathan's perspective.

Question 9. The Israelites held the New Moon festival at the beginning of each month to dedicate the month to God and to enjoy what God had provided. Celebrating while the moon was not visible protected them from worshiping the moon as some of the other nations did. Those attending the festival had to be ceremonially clean because a sacrifice would be offered to God. After washing their bodies and their clothes, they could participate in the sacrifice. For laws on ceremonial cleansing, see Leviticus 15 and Numbers 19:11-22.

Question 10. Shame is a powerful emotion that can destroy a person's self-respect. Encourage honest discussion about the pain of shame, but don't pressure anyone to speak about it if they are not ready.

STUDY 6: GROWING THROUGH FACING SIN

Note on 2 Samuel 11:1-27. Second Samuel 11:1 refers to spring as the time when kings went off to war. In the spring, after the winter rains, armies conducted their invasions on dry roads. The wheat and barley harvests provided food for the traveling army. Israel needed to defeat the powerful Ammonites, but King David sent Joab to lead the army instead of going himself. When Joab captured the Ammonite capital, he sent a message to David to come lead the army in the final siege of the city. "Otherwise I will take the city, and it will be named after me" (2 Samuel 12:26-28).

Question 2. Be sure the group discovers all the details. If necessary, ask, "Is there something else in verse…?"

Question 4. Try to recall times when you, unaware of any temptation, suddenly felt jealous, envious, angry, or lustful, or had other wicked thoughts.

Question 6. You might contrast David's response with your answers to question 1 to appreciate the difference.

Question 7. David, his family, and his nation suffered the consequences of his sin against God, the holy and righteous Judge. But they also received mercy and the privilege of being the physical ancestors of the Lord Jesus Christ.

Question 8. Make a list of all the verbs David used in his requests to see the scope of what he wanted God to do for him, and to appreciate what sin does to us. Perhaps it is because of the way he repented that God called David "a man after his own heart" (1 Samuel 13:14) and "my servant David, who kept my commands and followed me with all his heart, doing only what was right in my eyes" (1 Kings 14:8).

Question 12. If necessary, ask, "What are some of the things we do to convince God we are really sorry for our sin? What do we do to try to make ourselves worthy of forgiveness?"

Study 7: Growing Through Depression and Anger

Question 2. Jeremiah preached for God when Judah and Jerusalem were sent into captivity. The kings, princes, false prophets, priests, and people all railed against him and his unpopular message of repentance and judgment.

Allow time for a variety of responses to this question. Be sure the group discusses all the facts.

Question 3. God said that his word in Jeremiah's mouth would have both destructive and constructive consequences.

Question 5. God gave Jeremiah a preview of how royalty, priests, and people would oppose him. Ask the group to list specific as well as general problems they are currently facing and to think of a number of God's promises that offer encouragement in these circumstances. What happens when we aren't willing to face our problems realistically?

Questions 8–9. Three things upset Jeremiah: the prosperity of the wicked, the apparent indifference of the people to his preaching (Jeremiah 12:1), and the people's hypocrisy (verse 2). Jeremiah was willing to raise questions and to confront God about his seeming indifference to these conditions. God wanted Jeremiah to see that greater struggles loomed ahead (verse 5). "Men on foot" (foot soldiers) were the men of Anathoth. "Horses" (cavalry) represented the tough people in Jerusalem. "Safe country" represented village life. "Thickets by [or *the flooding of*] the Jordan" stood for more severe opposition in Jerusalem.

Question 10. Jeremiah had such an intimate walk with God that he could reveal his deepest hurts (Jeremiah 15:15). In verse 18, an Eastern metaphor—"a deceptive brook," "a spring that fails"—represents the trust that desert travelers placed in the oasis. If the oasis had no water, they were doomed. How does this analogy reveal Jeremiah's fear that God would fail him? Ask the group if they can think of other analogies.

Question 11. "Worthless words" (Jeremiah 15:19) refers to Jeremiah's accusation against God in verse 18.

Question 13. "Insult and reproach" (Jeremiah 20:8) is a low. "His word is in my heart like a fire" (verse 9) is a high. Help the group follow the pattern. Jeremiah ended on a profound low: "Cursed be the day I was born!" (verse 14).

Question 14. The idea of talking to God as Jeremiah did may repel some people and astonish others. For some, it's not part of the usual picture of the Christian experience. It may take some silent reflection before people in the group speak about this. Encourage the group to think of some positive growth experiences so that discussion does not end on a downer.

STUDY 8: GROWING THROUGH PRESSURE TO COMPROMISE

Question 2. Daniel, one of the Jewish captives educated in Babylon, so distinguished himself in all areas of learning that King Nebuchadnezzar gave him a high position in government. King Belshazzar succeeded his father, Nebuchadnezzar, but was killed by the Medes and Persians. When Darius the Mede became king over that vast empire, he planned to change the organizational chart.

Question 4. Consider what others might see in your attitudes, your responses to stress, whether or not you gossip, how you deal with conflict, and other actions, even if you are not verbal about your faith. The satraps must have watched Daniel carefully to conclude that they could not criticize him except for something related to his God. *Satrap* is from the old Persian word meaning "the protector of the realm." They held considerable power and had their own courts.

Question 6. Encourage the group to thoroughly discuss the options Daniel had and then consider how they might have weighed the pros and cons of each option before deciding what to do.

Question 8. The satraps didn't begin by announcing that Daniel had broken the decree. By first asking the question, they prompted the king to himself reaffirm the certainty of the decree. Only after hearing his affirmation did they announce that his most loyal administrator had violated the decree.

STUDY 9: GROWING THROUGH PERPLEXING SITUATIONS

Question 2. Habakkuk was a prophet in Judah when the Babylonians were replacing Assyria as the dominant world power. Both nations were known for their cruelty, military might, and proud idolatry.

In order to get all the facts, you may want to ask, "What else do you find in verse…?"

Question 3. The group may benefit from listing current examples of the evils Habakkuk recognized during his time. Also encourage them to reflect on unique issues in today's culture that trouble them.

Question 4. Habakkuk knew that the evil in Judah merited God's intervention. But for God to use the pagan Babylonians to punish his chosen people was unthinkable. Some of the unbelievable events among the nations to which God refers in Habakkuk 1:5 were: powerful Egypt was crushed; Nineveh, capital of Assyria, was plundered; Babylon rose to power; Judah was conquered and taken captive to Babylon.

Question 6. The ramparts or watchtower on the city walls enabled the watchman to see people approaching and to receive messengers. Habakkuk placed himself in the best position to see what God would say and do.

Everyone waits for something, but in different ways and

with different emotions. Encourage the group to think of specific situations in which their faith has changed how they wait.

Question 7. God would use proud, wicked Babylon to punish Judah, but in due time God would punish Babylon.

Question 8. Be sure the group sees the five accusations against the Babylonians, each introduced by "Woe to him..." (Habakkuk 2:6,9,12,15,19). Ask the group, "What do you learn about the Babylonians in verse 6...?"

Question 10. In contrast to the idol, which the worshiper tries unsuccessfully to awaken (Habakkuk 2:19), the Lord is awake and can hear and speak. So we can wait on God in confident, reverent silence.

Question 11. If there is time, reread Habakkuk 1:1-4 and 12-17, listening for Habakkuk's emotions. Then contrast these passages with chapter 3, especially verses 2 and 16-19.

Question 12. If the group needs help, ask, "What are the basic necessities in our society today, just as figs, grapes, olives, grain, sheep, and cattle were the basic necessities in Habakkuk's day?" No corn or wheat harvest? No gas for our cars?

Question 13. Encourage honest examples. If someone in the group is in a crisis, allow them freedom not to express their pain and impatience. Be prepared to give an example from your own life or about someone you know (with their permission, of course).

Study 10: Growing Through Failure

Question 2. Be sure the group sees the details of each part of the question. If necessary, ask, "Is there something else in verse...?"

Question 3. Encourage the group to put themselves in Peter's position. Think through the events and emotions of the evening. What would you say, or why would you have nothing to say?

Question 4. If we are aware of danger, we stay awake. If necessary, ask the group to think of a time they could hardly stay awake and then a child's cry or driving onto the highway shoulder jolted them fully awake.

Question 6. "Peter's words clearly identified him as a Galilean. Their accent was considered so ugly that no Galilean was allowed to pronounce the benediction at a synagogue service" (William Barclay, *The Gospel of Matthew*, vol. 2, Philadelphia: Westminister Press, 1958, p. 382).

Question 8. Ask the group to compare Peter's response to his sin with David's repentance in Psalm 51 (study 6).

Question 11. If necessary, ask, "How has Peter's view of himself changed since the time in the Upper Room? How has Peter's confidence in what Jesus knows changed?"

Peter had repented of his failure, but the shadow of his denial still hung over him. When Jesus asked three times if Peter loved him, Peter humbly confessed his love. He didn't boast or compare himself to the other disciples. Jesus lovingly reinstated Peter with new responsibilities because Peter really loved him, not because Peter was so strong.

STUDY 11: GROWING THROUGH WEAKNESS

Question 2. The false teachers in Corinth denied Paul's authority, questioned his motives, and accused him of weakness. The apostle responded by affirming his authority and giving a revolutionary view of weakness.

Question 3. Paul never specifically defined this thorn in the flesh, apparently a chronic and debilitating condition that hindered his ministry and travel. Some writers suggest he may have suffered from poor eyesight, malaria, epilepsy, or something that made his appearance repulsive.

Paul saw this thorn as a messenger of Satan but used by God for Paul's good and God's glory. The group may want to compare this with what they learned from Job's experience (study 4).

Question 4. Consider how long Paul might have waited to ask again. How might he have responded the first two times to God's refusal with no explanation? What questions might he have asked himself and God? What might Paul have said to Luke, his trusted doctor?

Questions 6–7. If necessary, consider what your first response to God's answer might be. How might you work through your disappointment to a place of acceptance?

Question 8. God has entrusted the treasure of the gospel to frail clay pots like Paul and like us to show that the power to change people's hearts belongs to him.

Question 10. Christ's death points to the need of daily self-denial—taking up our cross and following him. Jesus explained this principle in Mark 8:34, and Paul elaborated on it in Romans 6:11. Jesus' life in us makes it possible not to sin if we live under the control of the Holy Spirit (Romans 8:5-7).

STUDY 12: WHAT MAKES IT ALL POSSIBLE?

Question 2. Allow time for responses. Be sure all the facts are covered.

Question 3. The short, simple cry, "O Lord, save me," isn't eloquent, doesn't analyze the problem, and doesn't suggest a solution. But God hears this prayer.

Question 4. Review the answers to questions 2 and 3 to find similarities to the experiences of the group.

Question 5. Use the dictionary to define *gracious, righteous,* and *compassion.*

Question 6. If necessary, ask, "Why does it not say the *simple-minded?*" Use the dictionary to define *simple-hearted.*

Question 7. If necessary, ask, "What different emotions about death do you sense in Psalm 116:3,8, and 15?"

Question 8. The fear of death may be a threatening issue for some in the group. Allow freedom to speak honestly or to be silent.

Question 10. To "lift up the cup of salvation" (Psalm 116:13), the grateful worshiper stood before the altar, in sight of the people, and raised the cup of drink offering to celebrate his salvation. Be sure to put all of the responses in contemporary terms before you decide which ones you identify with.

Question 11. We may think that to repay God's goodness we must do something to make us worthy of it. But to repeatedly call on his goodness because we need it is wonderfully appropriate.

What Should We Study Next?

T o help your group answer that question, we've listed the Fisherman studyguides by category so you can choose your next study.

TOPICAL STUDIES

Angels by Vinita Hampton Wright

Becoming Women of Purpose by Ruth Haley Barton

Building Your House on the Lord: Marriage and Parenthood
by Steve and Dee Brestin

The Creative Heart of God: Living with Imagination
by Ruth Goring

Discipleship: The Growing Christian's Lifestyle by James and
Martha Reapsome

*Doing Justice, Showing Mercy: Christian Actions in Today's
World* by Vinita Hampton Wright

Encouraging Others: Biblical Models for Caring by Lin
Johnson

The End Times: Discovering What the Bible Says
by E. Michael Rusten

Examining the Claims of Jesus by Dee Brestin

Friendship: Portraits in God's Family Album by Steve and
Dee Brestin

The Fruit of the Spirit: Growing in Christian Character
by Stuart Briscoe

Great Doctrines of the Bible by Stephen Board

Great Passages of the Bible by Carol Plueddemann

Great Prayers of the Bible by Carol Plueddemann
Growing Through Life's Challenges by James and Martha
 Reapsome
Guidance & God's Will by Tom and Joan Stark
Heart Renewal: Finding Spiritual Refreshment by Ruth
 Goring
Higher Ground: Steps Toward Christian Maturity by Steve
 and Dee Brestin
*Images of Redemption: God's Unfolding Plan Through the
 Bible* by Ruth Van Reken
Integrity: Character from the Inside Out by Ted Engstrom
 and Robert Larson
Lifestyle Priorities by John White
Marriage: Learning from Couples in Scripture by R. Paul
 and Gail Stevens
Miracles by Robbie Castleman
One Body, One Spirit: Building Relationships in the Church
 by Dale and Sandy Larsen
The Parables of Jesus by Gladys Hunt
Parenting with Purpose and Grace by Alice Fryling
Prayer: Discovering What the Bible Says by Timothy Jones
 and Jill Zook-Jones
The Prophets: God's Truth Tellers by Vinita Hampton
 Wright
Proverbs and Parables: God's Wisdom for Living by Dee
 Brestin
Satisfying Work: Christian Living from Nine to Five
 by R. Paul Stevens and Gerry Schoberg
Senior Saints: Growing Older in God's Family by James and
 Martha Reapsome

The Sermon on the Mount: The God Who Understands Me
     by Gladys Hunt
Spiritual Gifts by Karen Dockrey
Spiritual Hunger: Filling Your Deepest Longings by Jim and
     Carol Plueddemann
A Spiritual Legacy: Faith for the Next Generation by Chuck
     and Winnie Christensen
Spiritual Warfare by A. Scott Moreau
The Ten Commandments: God's Rules for Living by Stuart
     Briscoe
Ultimate Hope for Changing Times by Dale and Sandy
     Larsen
Who Is God? by David P. Seemuth
Who Is Jesus? In His Own Words by Ruth Van Reken
Who Is the Holy Spirit? by Barbara Knuckles and Ruth Van
     Reken
Wisdom for Today's Woman: Insights from Esther by Poppy
     Smith
Witnesses to All the World: God's Heart for the Nations
     by Jim and Carol Plueddemann
Women at Midlife: Embracing the Challenges by Jeanie
     Miley
Worship: Discovering What Scripture Says by Larry Sibley

BIBLE BOOK STUDIES

Genesis: Walking with God by Margaret Fromer and
     Sharrel Keyes
Exodus: God Our Deliverer by Dale and Sandy Larsen
Ezra and Nehemiah: A Time to Rebuild by James Reapsome

(For Esther, see Topical Studies, *Wisdom for Today's Woman*)
Job: Trusting Through Trials by Ron Klug
Psalms: A Guide to Prayer and Praise by Ron Klug
Proverbs: Wisdom That Works by Vinita Hampton Wright
Ecclesiastes: A Time for Everything by Stephen Board
Jeremiah: The Man and His Message by James Reapsome
Jonah, Habakkuk, and Malachi: Living Responsibly
    by Margaret Fromer and Sharrel Keyes
Matthew: People of the Kingdom by Larry Sibley
Mark: God in Action by Chuck and Winnie Christensen
Luke: Following Jesus by Sharrel Keyes
John: The Living Word by Whitney Kuniholm
Acts 1–12: God Moves in the Early Church by Chuck and
    Winnie Christensen
Acts 13–28, see *Paul* under Character Studies
Romans: The Christian Story by James Reapsome
1 Corinthians: Problems and Solutions in a Growing Church
    by Charles and Ann Hummel
Strengthened to Serve: 2 Corinthians by Jim and Carol
    Plueddemann
Galatians, Titus, and Philemon: Freedom in Christ
    by Whitney Kuniholm
Ephesians: Living in God's Household by Robert Baylis
Philippians: God's Guide to Joy by Ron Klug
Colossians: Focus on Christ by Luci Shaw
Letters to the Thessalonians by Margaret Fromer and Sharrel
    Keyes
Letters to Timothy: Discipleship in Action by Margaret
    Fromer and Sharrel Keyes
Hebrews: Foundations for Faith by Gladys Hunt
James: Faith in Action by Chuck and Winnie Christensen

1 and 2 Peter, Jude: Called for a Purpose by Steve and Dee Brestin

How Should a Christian Live? 1, 2, and 3 John by Dee Brestin

Revelation: The Lamb Who Is a Lion by Gladys Hunt

BIBLE CHARACTER STUDIES

Abraham: Model of Faith by James Reapsome

David: Man After God's Own Heart by Robbie Castleman

Elijah: Obedience in a Threatening World by Robbie Castleman

Great People of the Bible by Carol Plueddemann

King David: Trusting God for a Lifetime by Robbie Castleman

Men Like Us: Ordinary Men, Extraordinary God by Paul Heidebrecht and Ted Scheuermann

Moses: Encountering God by Greg Asimakoupoulos

Paul: Thirteenth Apostle (Acts 13–28) by Chuck and Winnie Christensen

Women Like Us: Wisdom for Today's Issues by Ruth Haley Barton

Women Who Achieved for God by Winnie Christensen

Women Who Believed God by Winnie Christensen